Maple Syrup Poet

by
Vincent Costello

Strategic Book Publishing and Rights Co.

Copyright © 2012

All rights reserved—Vincent Costello

No part of this book may be reproduced or transmitted in any form or by any means, graphic, electronic, or mechanical, including photocopying, recording, taping, or by any information storage retrieval system, without the permission, in writing, from the publisher.

Strategic Book Publishing and Rights Co.
12620 FM 1960, Suite A4-507
Houston, TX 77065
www.sbpra.com

ISBN: 978-1-61897-162-3

Design: Dedicated Book Services, Inc. (www.netdbs.com)

Contents

Eternal Craving

A craving is all
A craving for honesty,
Like a child and his first
Plate of purple beets:
I'm stubborn

I surrender completely
Honesty embraces me unconditionally
Fear falls like orange
    October
    maple
    leaves

I'm no longer a soulfully ill child;
I am a golden eagle.

But don't be fooled;
My Herculean hair
Grows from
Vulnerability and humility.
It began with a craving.

Hometown Bound

My hometown has no use for me, I found
As brilliant as I am
As great an individual
To have around
—So they say

Which should bring a frown, to any man
Who is hometown bound
As time passes, you may find,
You're not so great to have around

Better off being a clown,
Better off in that western town

A sinner and a drunkard
Is more acceptable if you're hometown bound
—I have found

Leaking of the Gospel truth
Is hazardous to say the least;
You'll be shunned, persecuted silently
—Oh my, oh good grief
Can't seem to get no relief

But you know the truth:
Tribulation is the nature of this age,
Those married to Christ,
Have been there done that;
It was, and still is, all the rage

All things change.
But the truth,
Remains the same

Fight to stay there every day,
Keep clear of the great deception taking place,
Resist the insanity of the game

Peace, joy, and serenity
Is your reward:
Resist temptation
Eyes, on the Lord.

Bumble Bee

A bumble bee came to visit me today
She was just outside the window, as I sipped on my café
    Americano.
So lovely is the bumble bee, with her yellow and black coat
Like a tipsy toddler, she fluttered and danced about.
Mesmerized was I, of the magical qualities of the bumble
    bee.
She only stayed for a short time and off she went to visit a
    flower or two;
What words of wisdom did she have for me?
Be kind, gentle, and always remain humble, like the bumble
    bee,
Towards nature.
Thank you, lady bumble bee, you made my day.

Recipe for a Perfect Day

First, take surrendering your will freely,
To a Creator of your understanding
—One of pure goodness—
Stir in sunshine and blue skies
Mix in a sandy white beach and pleasant palm trees,
Pour in a turquoise sea teaming with life
—Especially sea horses—
Add a bay and rocky cliff,
Serve with a warm breeze and a leisurely
Stroll with someone you love with all your heart.

Cheer Up

Cheer up, lonely man
Things are not what they appear.
We're with you:
The angels and the Holy Ghost
So, chill dawg—you got nothing to fear

The plan is unfolding just as it should
I'm telling you gently,
Keep that self-will checked
And stay away from Hollywood

I'm trying to save as many as I can
You gotta believe me;
You and your loved ones
Even that wayward one "Stan"

So, cheer up, lonely man
Things are not as they appear
My plan as precise as a Rolex
Be patient;
Everything—in time
Will be made oh, so crystal clear

Keep loving me, and trusting me
With all your heart, soul, and mind

Love others as you love yourself
Be ever patient, tolerant, and kind.

Icy Fingers

Dreaming Canadian boy dreams
Hockey gods, 33, 66, and 99
It was no secret;
He would be all three combined

But then, sexual assault
Kicked off the summer
Any dreams he had became, a real bummer

Sexual assault takes its toll
But not in the same way,
As Keith Richards and rock and roll

Innocence victimized,
By the prince of this world
—Not the first, won't be the last—
You cannot go back and change things,
Cannot live in the past

Psychologists call it soul murder;
It wraps its icy fingers around the soul
And squeezes
—Oh so true

But there is a way out;
Of this, you can have no doubt,
My friend,
Before you reach for that rope
Here's some good dope

You can confront the soul murderer
One day at a time,
Bring him into the light,
Despises the light, despises what's right

Laura Davis and *Courage to Heal*
Will take you gently there,
She will lay your abuse to bare
—With great care

It helps to let go of control,
To become vulnerable,
To the healing balm of the light as a whole

Like a caterpillar and her cocoon
The Creator will be with you every day
Car-ry-ing you, when nerves begin to fray

So stay—here on earth—
Prepare yourself, for an amazing new birth
A new you:
Full of richness and mountains of worth.

The Phony House

Welcome mental illness, welcome you all
Welcome to our place of restoration
We'll happily embrace you
We promise to be open and true.

Drink in the ambience
Of our happy-go-lucky abode
Be at peace, my friend,
You've struck the mother lode

Psst, psst friend:
Do not expect us to be real
That's too much to ask;
Expecting us to feel and be real is a daunting task.

Just expect that we'll love you,
But not really love you:
A concept simple for you to embrace
Even if it makes us seem shallow
And open to ridicule, plus disgrace.

Fall in love with one of us? Never!
Stick to your own kind
We're the well, you see, you're the mentally ill

Fuck man,
Are you blind?

Love is beneath us;
You see, here we make the rules
Besides, love is passé
It's for the idiots and the fools

It's not spoken, but hell, you gotta understand
That there are two separate wants and desires here
One for me, another for you
Man.

So, we welcome you
But we don't welcome you
So get that through your sick head
You can do it; it's easy
But then again, there's always the street instead.

I'm Not Al Capone

Hello stranger
Why so afraid?
I'm not Al Capone
Nor the embodiment of a can of Raid

The separation between us
What is it, my friend?
Like two continents pulling away
Never to be together, again

Apples and oranges get along
Better than you and me
A squirrel and his acorn
Love each other deeper
—While sitting atop
That ol' elm tree

Phony love,
Is what we seem to believe in these days
Deep, committed love
Is a stranger we view with contempt:
"What you talkin' 'bout Willis?"
Have you been sampling,

More of that, BC hemp?

Nope: don't smoke that dope
True love being replaced with phony love
Less work, more manageable they say,
You can pick it up
Off any drive thru tray

Integrity, decency, and hope:

Well, their being subjected
To a full body scan
A game changer's coming
Top up the oil in your lamp

Doubt me?
Look what happened to Haiti and Japan.

Political Correctness

Living in a world of political correctness
Don't subscribe to the lie,
How it ain't gonna affect us

One day you'll wake up:
Ain't gonna see no more Texas
Or be driving no cool,
Mother fucking looking Lexus

Islam, Buddhism, Christianity:
We don't really believe in shit no more
We so busy making accommodations
Shit man, we ain't got no more core

Gay rights, feminism rights
They all driving their own agenda
Who are we? Who the fuck's the kids
We once called Jack and Brenda?

New ageism, humanism,
They all marching to their own sweet drummer
Where you fit in? What suit you wearing?
The blue one?
Or the one Oprah thinks is a God damn hummer

Too many beliefs
Something's got to give
The truth must shine through
For humanity to thrive and live

Where's the hope in this sea of vanilla
Could it be the Prince of Peace?
Is he the fella?

Hope so:
Someone like Superman
Must grab humanity by the collar
Elsewise,
Pretty soon, we'll be fucking worth,
Much less than a dollar.

Bed Sores of Hate

What's on my plate?
Twenty-seven-year-old bed sores of hate
That was my unwanted family heirloom,
That was my tragic fate,
This twenty-seven-year-old bed sores of hate

War zones do not only exist
In a conventional light,
Often—quite often—they're hidden
Completely out of sight

Our Canadian troops march
To fight a war over there;
But the war is everywhere,
Barely any man, woman, and child
Has been left to spare

Twenty-seven-year-old bed sores of hate,
Eventually, will tear your life to shreds,
Bankrupting your soul, tossing U aside,
Leaving U to rot,
On large quantities of meds

The seventeenth-century Spanish ships
Had to have a noble captain and first mate
To steer themselves out of trouble
I did too,
To navigate my way—out and away—
From the bed sores of hate bubble

Canadian old-age cheddar
Requires patience, care, and time
Before it gets better

15

Freeing yourself from bed sores of hate
Mirrors the journey of old-age cheddar:
Requires patience, care, and time
Before the soul gets better

It's not like mailing a local letter

The odyssey can begin:
With a simple, help me please God
I'm sick and tired of living with
twenty-seven-year-old bed sores of hate

I want them gone!
Completely off my plate
Before it's too late!

small penis men

I'd like to talk about the penis
Can we talk about the penis in Canada?

Good God, no.
We can't talk about the penis in Canada
I don't hear too many men or women
Talking 'bout the penis
At the Tim Horton Donut Coffee Shop

U can talk about hockey in Canada
Ya, hockey's okay,
Just, not the penis

U can talk about the penis in France
Ya, in France it's okay

Can we talk about the vagina in Canada?

Good God, no.
We can't talk about the vagina in Canada

U can talk 'bout the vagina in France
Ya, in France it's okay

I don't recall there ever being
A course in high school on
How to lick a vagina properly
Nope, I can't remember

I think I would have been
In the thick of that line up
Had there been such a course, I really do

I remember signing up for
Science, math, and history
But I don't remember
Signing up for a course
On how to lick a vagina properly

I think Canadian men
Would have benefited greatly
From such a course

Don't U think?

But back to the penis,
'Cause that's what we're here to talk about

I . . . have a small penis
Are there any other men out there
Who also have a small penis?
Not too many hands going up

Are there any men out there,
Who have a small penis
But can't admit to others that
They, have a small penis?
Not too many hands going up

Finally, are there any men out there who
Talk as if and tell others that they
Have a huge penis?
A few heads nodding

I . . . have a Volkswagen Beetle for a penis
Ya, fortunately, woman love Volkswagen Beetles
Ya, 'cause they're cute, fun to drive, and they can go a long
Way on a tank of gas
—fairly nimble in and out of traffic, good in tunnels

Oh sure, I admire the Mack truck penis
What small penis man wouldn't?
Ron Jeremy has a Mack truck penis
You ever seen that?
I've seen it; it's definitely a Mack truck penis

Of course, the most awesome penis of them all
Is the 747 penis
Elephants have 747 penises
You ever seen that?
I have; I watch those wildlife shows
It's definitely a 747 penis

Oh my goodness
There's a woman and a man in the audience
That wouldn't mind having a 747 penis
Be . . . careful what U wish for

There are other advantages to having
A Volkswagen Beetle penis
For example, a 747 penis man
Well, he will often induce a woman to scream in terror
A Volkswagen Beetle penis man, on the other hand,
Will only induce a woman to laughter, I know

A 747 penis man will often have to
Tie his penis around his leg once or twice
A Volkswagen penis man?
Well, he can't reach his leg, I know

Finally, a 747 penis man while
Riding up an escalator—in busy shopping mall—
On a Saturday afternoon
Well, he may trip and fall
And ouch, that hurts

A Volkswagen Beetle penis man
Well, he would never be riding
Up an escalator—in a busy shopping mall—
On a Saturday afternoon
No, he's too humble, embarrassed, and shy; I know

So, summing things up
I, have a small penis
And I will go through the rest of my life with a small penis

Small penis men of Canada be proud!
Small penis men of the world unite
Oppose and fight gallantly
The huge penis men of the world

And who knows;
In my next life, I may get a 747 penis
Be . . . careful what U wish for.

Acne on My Ass

I have acne on my ass
And I don't know what to do about it

I've studied it—I've looked at my ass
In the mirror—I picked a few,
While looking at my ass in the mirror
With only my ass looking back at me

Are there any acne ass pickers out there
Who have experienced this?
I know you're out there
It's quite hidden and not hidden
This acne on our ass situation

The media, well, they focus on the
Murderers, the terrorists, and the
Dirty sleazy politicians
But they don't focus on the truth:
And that's this acne on our ass situation
It's epidemic and threatening to grow even further

There's a lot more acne on our asses
Out there, than we care to talk about
But back to the acne on my ass

So, I went to see the pharmacist
And I said, "I'd like some shit for this
Acne on my ass situation,"
And that cleared the store some

The pharmacist said,
"You can't say that in here;
No, this is a politically correct store
And that's not allowed."

So I said, "What the fuck should I call it then?"
He said, "Call it a skin condition."
You see, there's a lot of denial out there

So, me being me, I said,
"Can I get some stuff for this acne on my ass/skin condi-
    tion?"
He threw me out of the store

So, I found a pharmacist who wasn't politically correct

And got some shit for this acne on my ass situation

So, hopefully in a few weeks' time
Things will have cleared up
Because I'm a forward-looking guy
I decided to start a twelve-step program
For acne ass sufferers
Will call it: Acne Ass Sufferers Anonymous
AASA for short

Hopefully, one acne ass sufferer at a time
We can make this world a better place.

A Reckoning a Coming

This is good dope,
The best U ever had,
The dope to make U happy,
The dope to make U sad

There's a reckoning a coming
A settling of accounts,
Even though U are uncertain,
Even though U have your doubts

The Son of man—who U all know well—
Is not far away, and it's gonna be swell,
But before he arrives, we'll be going through hell

Pray you'll be blessed as blessed can be
You and your loved ones,
Both U and me

The story is old and you're familiar with him too,
Son of dawn, Giver of light,
Lucifer, is a fancy name now

Listen all and listen well:
For the prince of this world's reign is a coming to an end
His plan is a going straight to hell

Coming back for a return engagement,

Coming back to set up shop
Is the Prince of Peace:
None other than Jesus Christ
—To some he's just Pop

Thugs and lovers of evil ways
Your reign is coming to an end,
Your history of leading so many innocent astray,
Will no longer be a growing trend

The King of king's patience is wearing thin,
He's sick and tired of those who sneer
And show great contempt for sin

There's a reckoning a coming, a settling of accounts
Even though U are uncertain,
Even though U have your doubts

Upon Christ's return
A celebration will take place:
Mother T, Emily Carr, and Emily Dickenson will be in the
     house,
Martin Luther and Gandhi too
The Walrus, Tupac, Elvis, Janis Joplin, and Billie Holiday
Will sing a tune or two

As far as the eyes can see:
We'll be blessed to look upon the Lord of lord's face;
While many others will stand outside
The Kingdom, in utter disgrace

Perhaps, it's time to make a choice
Just who's fucking side are U on:
The side of life or the side of death,
The side that sucks your blood,
Or the side that gives U breath

Perhaps, it's time to turn to the Gospels
The truth U crave, well, it's there
The clock till judgment time is ticking
U ain't—got fucking time to spare
There's a reckoning a coming, a settling of accounts
Even though U are uncertain, even though U have your
      doubts.

Waves

Waves, waves, waves
Waves come in, waves go out
Waves come in, waves go out
Come in, go out
In, out

I can't live without waves
I can't live without waves

My life is a wave
My relationship's a wave

Waves say hello, waves say goodbye
Waves say hello, waves say goodbye
Say hello, say goodbye
Hello, goodbye

Waves are true, they always come back to U
Waves are true, they always come back to U

Birth, death
Birth, death

Waves, waves, waves.

Please God, If You Are There

Well, it was hot and muggy, but what do you expect? Summers were like this every year, no big deal. My name is Jimmy, I'm twelve years old, and this is what happened to me three days after my dad died suddenly of an aneurysm.

"What's an aneurysm?" I asked my older sister, Rose. She told me an artery near his heart popped inside of him, and the doctors tried but couldn't fix him.

"Holy Moses," I said, "I hope nothing pops near my heart. What's an artery?"

I remember being at the funeral home and it was weird. They made me kneel in front of my dad's dark green coffin—I thought green was a cool color—but the weirdest part was you could see my dad in the coffin. Real spooky you know. Dad had lost a lot of weight, and he had make-up on too, I could tell. Also, there was a rosary hanging from his hands, and his hands were crossed together on his stomach. I was curious, so I grabbed one of his fingers and picked it up. Weird, his finger was an orangey color underneath, and it was cold and stiff too. The dead sure look different when they're dead and not alive. He wasn't breathing I could tell; he was dead for sure. After I pretend prayed, I got up and went back to my chair. Rose gave me heck for pulling on his finger. Heck was my middle name, I think.

"Just curious," I said. She just rolled her eyes.

The next day, we all went to the church, where most of my sister's sang songs in the choir and lots of people cried, girls mostly. Then there were more prayers and songs at the gravesite. If you ask me, I don't think funerals are much fun really. I think the fair and the ride's there are much better. Later, loads of people drove back to our place.

"Don't go too far, Jimmy," my mom said after we left the car we used to go to the graveyard. "Pretty soon we'll be eating lunch, so stick around."

"Okay, I hear ya, Mom," I said. But I didn't really hear her. I was not good at taking orders. I questioned too much, they told me. I loosened my bow tie and the top three buttons on my dress shirt. Being held captive by my tie was no fun; I didn't enjoy being held captive by anything.

I was more shocked by my dad's death than anything, and I felt relief too. My dad was crazy for a long time, I think. He wasn't drinking anymore, but he still scared the be-Jesus out of me.

My dad was Irish Catholic, and not any Catholic I liked, that's for sure. I remember you had to be perfect around my dad, and even that wasn't good enough. He was such a control freak, and I remember lots of yelling and getting beat up a lot. I feared for my life around my dad, which never felt right to me. I remember thinking I was gonna die one time, when I was eleven. I fooled around too much at Mass, and boy did I get it. He pulled me down to the basement and took the wooden end of the plunger to my bum. I felt I was gonna die that day.

Another time, he made me watch as he beat my two brother's with the belt. My mother tried to pull him away by grabbing my dad by the hair. It didn't stop him; I watched helplessly as my brother's got the licking. I remember thinking to myself, *I can't believe this is my family. Please God, if you are there, can I have another family please?* I know there was love somewhere inside my dad, but at the time he died, I could only think, *Thanks God, if you are there, for taking away this bully, who didn't seem like my father at all.*

I think I liked my mother much better. She was gentle and had feeling. She was French and Indian, I heard. We didn't talk much about my mom's side of the family. Things would have been much worse without Mom around. I think God sent her as an angel, maybe.

"Hey Jimmy, were you at a wedding or something?" asked my friend, Keith, the next door neighbor who was watching us from his front steps.

"Nah," I said, "I was just at my dad's funeral. He died a couple of days ago."

"Oh geez," Keith said. "I'm real sorry; I didn't know."

"No big deal." I was always saying no big deal, even if it was a big deal. "It was kind of sudden eh; he was sick for awhile, and then now he's gone."

My family and I lived in social housing. I was ashamed of where I lived. We laughed and called it the Boullee ghetto. The kids at school seemed to come from much better homes and dressed better than me. I didn't like rich kids much. Everybody in the city seemed richer than my family and me. There were about seven or eight town houses where I lived, stuck together. Many of the kids didn't have dads where I lived. The rest of the family showed up as I was talking to Keith.

"Come on, Jimmy," my mom said. "Let's get inside." I remember my mom looked angry when she talked to me.

"See you around," Keith said. I turned and ran into the house.

My mom hated me hanging around with Keith. She told me to stay away from the next door people. Keith was two years older than I was and had a few nasty-looking tattoos. He also used a lot of swear words, smoked red-packaged DuMaurier cigarettes, and sold some drugs. As well, he had spent some time in a detention center. The bad stuff didn't seem to bother me much. I thought Keith was cool, really. He came from a bad home just like me. He seemed nice, just did bad things I guess.

The next day I met up with Keith. We met up in the courtyard that was inside the town houses. I was trying out the new slide that was just put in.

"Hey Jimmy, fuck man, what's shaking?" he said.

"Ah, not much," I said. "Kind of bored, I guess."

"Ya, I get bored too. Around here, it's easy to get bored. Listen buddy, I got a plan that might interest ya. Want to hear it?"

"Sure."

"Well, a couple of buddies plus me are going pool-hopping tonight, and you're invited too. Fuck man, it'll be a blast. What do ya say?"

I didn't know what to say. I had heard about pool-hopping from the other kids, but dared not to think about it even, with Dad around. Things were different now.

"Okay, I'm in."

"Beauts buddy, put it here. Just meet me outside your backyard fence at midnight."

I couldn't tell my mom of course; I couldn't tell no one. The day went way too slow after that. I could think of little else besides the pool-hopping. I saw the danger. There were signs posted outside the pool: Trespassers Will Be Prosecuted. I remember seeing those big signs. But none of that mattered much really. Dad was gone, and now I could do what I wanted, at least that's what I thought. I could be a rebel like Keith if I wanted too. It was my turn to run the show.

There were other reasons for me to be excited about pool-hopping. I didn't have a lot of friends, so maybe these guys could be my friends. I knew they were into bad ways, but at least I was wanted by somebody. I never felt I got enough love at home, really. Mom and Dad never had enough time just for me. Six kids at home was too many, I think. Also, some of us at home were more favorite to Dad and Mom, and that didn't include me. Nah, I was always causing trouble it seemed. "Here comes trouble," I heard more than once. So, even if my new friends were known as outlaws in the neighborhood, they were okay with me.

Later that night, the pool-hopping plans seem to hit a bump. Somehow, my brother Paul found out about the plans, and the turncoat blabbed it to Mom. I found out at supper time.

"Jimmy," my mom said. "I don't want you pulling any boners, by going pool-hopping tonight, do you hear." That always made me laugh when Mom said that word *boners*.

"Pool-hopping," I said. "Where did you hear about that?" Paul was sitting across the table, grinning from ear to ear.

"Never mind who told me. They'll be no fooling around tonight. Just because your father's gone, doesn't mean all hell is gonna break loose, all right, mister?"

"Okay Mom, whatever you say." I was blazing mad at my brother Paul. I gave him a murderous look. He was always tattling on me.

After supper, I sat on the front steps of our town house. I was depressed. Why was my brother Paul not on my side? He and my older brother, Mark, always seemed to enjoy getting me into trouble. How come I couldn't trust them? How come I couldn't have a brother who was close to me, who understood me? Why isn't the world like I want it to be? Oh God, if you are there, you are so cruel.

After everyone had gone to sleep that night, I laid wide awake in my bed—I always had trouble sleeping at night, not sure why. Across the room, my brother Paul was already asleep. I was wondering, *Now that Dad's gone, who's gonna look after the family? Who will take his place?* Mark probably. He already had his own room, and had been Dad's favorite for a long time. Mark enjoyed being the boss and looked most Irish like Dad too. Is fourteen a normal age to be a dad?

I started thinking about the pool-hopping again. *I really want to go and nothing is going to stop me*, I thought. I waited till the clock on my night table said 11:50, and then I checked to see if Paul was still sleeping. Then I got out of bed and dressed into my swimming trunks that were close by. Then I made my way to the bathroom, as quietly as that black panther in that *Jungle Book* movie I had seen. I flushed the toilet and the whooshing sound made it so I could escape to the basement. I got nervous, as some of the stairs creaked on my way down to the basement. Luckily, Mom didn't wake up though. When I got to the basement, everything was pitch dark. Fear was with me in the basement. It was in this place where I had to witness my brother's being whipped by the belt. The whippings always matched our age; don't know why. In the basement is where my dad beat me with the wooden end of the plunger, after Mass one Holy Sunday. Maybe Dad was trying to beat the devil out of me, I don't know.

I eventually made my way to the only lonely-looking window, grabbed onto the two cement washing sinks, and pulled myself up with ease. I was getting excited for sure. The window came out easy. I had done this before; I was getting good at it. I reached for the window after I was secure and inside the window well, placed it back, and shut it gently. It stayed shut, even without the latch. Bonus! I turned around to face the backyard; I felt the uneven rocks at the bottom of the window well. I pulled myself up and out of the well and onto the dewy grass. I could hear the grasshoppers chirping—nice sound.

"Hey Jimmy, pssst, pssst," Keith's voice whispered loudly. I could hear him, but because of the darkness, I couldn't place the voice. Suddenly, I saw the blonde head of hair peering around the backyard fence. I stayed low as I ran quickly to meet him. I was giddy with joy, but kept it silent.

"Hey, how's it going, man?" Keith said. He had a big grin on too.

"I'm good," I said. "Where's the other guys?"

"They're at the pool, man, so let's peel."

Cool. We were actually on our way. I felt free and my heart was pounding like mad; we ran quickly. The pool was not far from our town houses. The pool was run by the city, and it was next to a grade school. Behind the pool was a big field. It only took a couple of minutes to get to the pool. It looked so different at nighttime. I didn't know what it felt like to be a criminal, but I think what I was feeling is what criminals feel when they first start their careers. I could hear some splashing and the sound of the diving board as we neared the pool.

Once we got to the pool fence, Keith laughed and blurted out, "Hey man, what the fuck are you two doing trespassing?"

It was local tough guy, Ralph, who answered. "Keep it down, Keith, we don't want anyone calling the fuzz," he said.

The other local kid in on the pool-hopping action was Ted. "Yeah, you little dickhead," he laughed, "keep it down."

Keith and I climbed the fence as fast as possible. Man, to see the diving pool in the dark was really cool. I knew the other two boys a little. Ralph was somebody I was always afraid of kinda. I think he was well known by the cops and, like Keith, had spent time at a juvenile detention place. Ralph commanded respect by not even saying anything; it's just the way it was with him. Ted was a real joker; he didn't scare me much. Kinda reminded me of the scarecrow in the movie, *The Wizard of Oz*.

"How's it going, Ralph?" I was trying to sound tough.

"Not bad, not bad," he said coolly. "This is your first time, eh Jimmy? Are you ready for some fun?"

"Oh ya for sure." I was happy Ralph talked to me. I needed friends, lots of friends.

"Hey watch this," Keith said as he climbed up onto the diving board. "Scooby dooby doo." I heard him say as he ran, bounced, and then twisted his body in midair, before splashing down into the water. I followed him up onto the diving board. Everything was so dark I could hardly see the water. I was cautious and took my time; I wanted to dive like the pros.

"Just run and dive, jackass," Ted said. He didn't bother me much. I took three careful steps, bounced, and gave my best effort at a dive in the pike position. Just as I entered the water I somersaulted. I loved the feeling that came to my head from the somersault. The water was warm, warmer than it was during the day. I reached the surface.

"How do you like it, buddy?" Keith said as he splashed water at me.

"Pretty awesome," I said, "can't see a thing down there."

"Fuck. Not supposed to see a thing, man, that's what makes it so cool. Yepper pepper, dude."

I didn't understand what yepper pepper meant. Keith was always saying it though. It had a nice ring to it, I thought— sort of like music. It meant fun, I guess. For the next twenty minutes or so, the four of us laughed, made fun of each other, and took turns on the diving board. Each kid tried to do something more fancy off the board than the other. I knew what happiness was. Up 'til now, happiness was a stranger I only knew a little. Then the fun was broken.

"Hey you guys, where's that light coming from?" Ted yelled." Man is that bright." He saw the light just as I was jumping off the board.

When I broke the surface, Keith was yelling at me in a whispered tone. "C'mon Jimmy," he said. "The cops are here; get out and follow me."

I started to panic and felt the way I did whenever I knew I was gonna get it from my crazy dad. I didn't like these feelings. I swam to the side of the pool fast, got out, and followed Keith to the back fence. Ralph was already over the fence and running across the open field. Keith and I were not far behind. As I was running, to who knows where, I looked behind me. I could see the cop running after us and boy was I scared. Pretty soon, Keith and I were lucky to find some trees and then we darted into some bushes. Ralph kept running ahead of us.

In seconds, I heard the sound of the cop's boots as he ran right by Keith and I, and after Ralph. We scrunched up close to the bushes as water dripped off our bodies. We looked wide-eyed at each other and laughed quietly as we both shivered. The laughter was covering the scared feelings we both felt.

"Geez, Keith, I think were fucked," I said. I wasn't really a swearer, but it made me feel bigger to swear.

"No dude, we're all right," Keith said. "Just stay quiet, and he won't find us."

Please God, I thought, *if you are there, can you get me out of this?* I needed to go pee, but I couldn't risk standing up, so I held it. Seemed like we waited forever, but then we could hear some voices. It was Ralph and the cop, and they were coming closer to our hiding place.

"Do you know where those two went?" the cop asked.

"No, I was way ahead of them," Ralph said. He talked coolly with the cop, almost as if they knew each other. Keith and I could hear the sound of something moving through the bushes we were hiding behind. It was some sort of stick being used by the cop. I had wished my heart would slow down; I was really scared.

"Okay, you guys!" the cop shouted. "I know you're around here somewhere. If you don't come out, I'm gonna call the dogs in, and they'll sniff you out. So it's up to you; either you come out now or the dogs will get ya."

Well, I guess that did it for me. Something spoke to me—I heard my mother call it my conscience. I stood up from the security of the bushes.

"I give up, sir," I said. Ralph looked down and shook his head. I had failed miserably at being a criminal.

"What a goofball," Keith said, as he gave up too. I told the policeman I had to go pee, and he let me run to the nearest tree.

Later on, the three of us sat shaking in the backseat of the police car, while the policeman wrote some stuff down and talked to someone on the radio. It was my first time in a police car, and I didn't like the feelings I was having. Keith and Ralph were more cool; they were used to the police car, I guess. *Where did Ted go?* I thought. I was too scared to ask the policeman where he was.

"Okay boys," the policeman said, "I'm gonna take you all home now. You're gonna have to go to court in the future for this stunt you pulled tonight. You'll be hearing from us. Safe to say, I don't want to see you fellas in the backseat of my car again. You got me?"

"Yes, sir," Keith and I said. Ralph kept silent. Turns out, Ted wasn't such a scarecrow from the *Wizard of Oz* after all. The next day, I found out he stayed behind in the pool area while the rest of us ran across the field. Then he high-tailed it home. I laughed when I heard the story the next day.

I didn't want the policeman to take me home. I would have been happier swallowing a sandwich of cockroaches, really. If only he would let me sneak in through the window well, everything would be fine. The policeman knocked on my door and Rose answered. She looked half asleep.

"Good evening, Officer," she said politely. What's the problem?"

"Well," said the officer, "this little guy here says this is his home."

"Oh Jimmy, what did you get yourself into?"

I remember hearing things like *troublemaker* and *bad boy*. Even though she laughed, I didn't like the names she called me. I was always being called a bad boy. I didn't want to hear those things. Somewhere deep down, I knew I wasn't those things. *If I was, my family was making me into a bad boy, a troublemaker,* I thought. I was just trying to have some fun and be free. Dad never let me be free. Besides, boys are dare doers; that's what we do.

The next day, my mom gave me heck, but she laughed along with Rose and the others in the family. Being brought home by the cops was something to laugh about, I guess. Later that day, as I was heading to the variety store to get Mom some milk and bread, I thought about things. I was always thinking about things, always serious about life even though I was just a kid. I didn't enjoy causing grief for Mom. It was a tough time for her already with losing Dad and all; although I think Mom was a little relieved that Dad was dead. I could sense it as I watched her reaction to his death. He made her life miserable for a long time, I think.

Hanging around with Keith and his buddies maybe wasn't such a good idea, but where was I gonna get my friends from? *Dear God, if you are there, maybe you could help me figure things out. I can't do this on my own; I need all the help I can get.*